Experiencing God's Love in a Broken World—

A Spiritual Journey

ENDORSEMENTS

Here is a great resource for Christians who want to go deeper ... for believers who long for greater intimacy with their Creator."
—**Nick Harrison**, author of *Magnificent Prayer, His Victorious Indwelling*, and *Power in the Promises*.

In this world of confusion and uncertainty, discovering a road map to know God's love and understand yourself is refreshing. Theologically sound and simply stated, *Experiencing God's Love in a Broken World* is truth to guide your life. I recommend traveling with Roy and Deb Haggerty on this spiritual journey of knowing God and living for him.
—**Dave Beckwith**, Western US Regional Director for Standing Stone Ministries, senior pastor emeritus Woodbridge Church, Irvine, CA

Years ago, as a new believer going through an incredibly difficult time, I heard someone say, "God is good ... all the time." My head sensed that was true, but my heart wasn't convinced. Then someone else told me, "Life is difficult ... but God is good." It took me many years to truly lay hold of that great truth, but once I did, it was an amazingly freeing experience. *Experiencing God's Love in a Broken World* by Roy and Deb Haggerty is a book I wish I'd had in those early years, as it would certainly have helped me absorb this powerful principle of God's goodness, regardless of circumstances. I highly recommend this book to anyone experiencing a difficult time of their own—or to those who simply want a closer, more intimate relationship with their Lord.
—**Kathi Macias**, author of more than fifty books, including Golden Scrolls 2011 Novel of the Year, *Red Ink*.

Experiencing God's Love in a Broken World presents theological concepts of the Gospel and sanctification in understandable and interesting ways so that Christians know what to believe, why they should believe, and the significance

of believing. As lay counselors, we look forward to passing along this book to add another layer of mentoring for those who come to us with life issues.
—**Larry Miller**, author of *Men of the Bible*, and **Kathy Collard Miller,** author of *Pure-Hearted: The Blessings of Living Out God's Glory*

Experiencing God's Love in a Broken World by Roy and Deb Haggerty provides a helpful handbook filled with solid theology told in an understandable manner.
—**James N. Watkins**, award-winning author and Bible teacher

Roy and Deb Haggerty's *Experiencing God in a Broken World* is a wonderful guide for both the seeker and the believer. Reading the biblical truths within these pages produced two responses within me. The renewed desire to love God with all my heart, soul, and strength, and an urgency to tell others of his agapé love. I will keep this resource on hand, ready to gift to those who come to me for counsel. Of course, I'll keep a personal copy to read and read again and again and again …
—**Shelley Pierce,** author, *Sweet Moments: Insight and Encouragement for the Pastor's Wife*

Experiencing God's Love in a Broken World by Roy and Deb Haggerty is a bright light in a dim world. Their clear thinking and warm hearts are trustworthy guides in the maze of life. They take complex issues—that matter—and take your hand and walk through them with you. Can't wait to get the book—and share with others.
—**Dixie Fraley Keller**, author, the *Widows' Workbook*, Bible teacher.

At age 18, I repeated the Sinner's Prayer, following the young man who'd patiently shared Jesus with me for months. I knew very little other than God loved me and sent Jesus to die for me. In the moment, that was enough. But soon, I longed for answers about Jesus and the Bible and desired to know what my new life in Christ entailed. Had Roy and Deb Haggerty's book, *Experiencing God's Love in a Broken World—A Spiritual Journey*, been placed in my hands, how different, how much deeper, those early years could have been. The Haggertys share their decades long walk with Jesus in an easy to understand and quick to internalize volume of work. This book will be close by as a resource in our ministry for those desiring to live—and understand—God's word fully.
—**Deb DeArmond**, author, *Related by Chance, Family by Choice*

EXPERIENCING GOD'S LOVE IN A BROKEN WORLD

Experiencing God in a Broken World provides readers with a formula for Christian growth that transforms faith from a concept into a lifestyle. These short but detailed chapters provide a roadmap for a spiritual walk that is timeless in application as it continually connects readers to a God who is a real, dynamic, and vibrant presence even in a chaotic world.
—**Ace Collins,** author, *In the President's Service* series, *Stories Behind the Hymns that Inspire America*

In *Experiencing God in a Broken World,* the subjects and order of the chapters take the reader on a progressive journey that demonstrates how learning more about our loving Heavenly Father yields a deeper desire to worship Him. This is a resource I will keep in my spiritual toolbox and will re-read many times and refer to often.
—**Jennifer Kopald**, author and speaker, *The Beast and the Beauty of Breast Cancer*

I had the opportunity to read an early version of *Experiencing God's Love in a Broken World*. I shared the content with my family. We found the concepts gave us much to think about and discuss. Anyone who wants to have a more intimate relationship with God will benefit from reading this book.
—**Dell R. Hyssong, Jr.**, pastor and member of the award-winning Hyssongs gospel music trio

Experiencing God's Love in a Broken World—

A Spiritual Journey

Roy Haggerty

with

Deb Haggerty

PUBLISHING THE POSITIVE

ELK LAKE PUBLISHING INC
Plymouth, Massachusetts

Copyright Notice

Experiencing God's Love in a Broken World—A Spiritual Journey

Cover and Interior Design: Derinda Babcock

Editor: Deb Haggerty

PUBLISHED BY: Elk Lake Publishing, Inc., Plymouth, MA 02360, 2019

Library Cataloging Data

Names: Haggerty, Roy and Deb (Roy and Deb Haggerty)

Experiencing God's Love in a Broken World—A Spiritual Journey / Roy and Deb Haggerty

118 p. 23cm × 15cm (9in × 6 in.)

Description: A mentoring program designed for people who have been Christians for a while, who wish to know God more intimately and desire to serve him more effectively. What could be more awesome than loving more deeply the One who created us for that very purpose?

Identifiers: ISBN-13: 978-1-950051-74-8 (trade) | 978-1-950051-75-5 (POD) |978-1-950051-76-2 (e-book.)

Key Words: mentoring, spiritual growth, free will, discipleship, personal growth, inspirational, self-image

LCCN: 2019xxxxx Nonfiction

To our loving God, who loved us first and created us to love him with all our hearts, minds, souls, and strength.

Contents

Acknowledgments xi

INTRODUCTION 1

PROLOGUE 3

CHAPTER ONE: WHO DO WE SAY GOD IS? 5

Our Theology: 5

God's Revelation of Himself in Creation 6

God's Revelation of Himself through the Bible. 6

God's Revelation of Himself in Jesus 8

Questions for Thought 11

CHAPTER TWO: GOD'S RELATIONSHIP WITH US 15

What Does the Bible Tell Us? 15

Questions for Thought 21

CHAPTER THREE: OUR PERSONAL RELATIONSHIP WITH GOD. . .23

Do We, Personally, Have a Loving Relationship with God? 23

Questions for Thought 29

CHAPTER FOUR: WHO ARE WE? 31

Who Do We Say We Are? 31

God's Sovereignty and Man's Free Will 32

Understanding Free Will 35

Questions for Thought 40

CHAPTER FIVE: WHO DOES GOD SAY WE ARE? 43

What Is Our Response 45

Questions for Thought 48

CHAPTER SIX: HOW DO WE CONNECT WITH GOD 51

Prayer 51

Worship 53

The Ministry of the Holy Spirit. 54

Questions for Thought 55

CHAPTER SEVEN: WHY ARE WE HERE? 57

What is Our Purpose? 57

How Do We Discover Our Assignments from God? 60

Questions for Thought 63

CHAPTER EIGHT: CALL TO ACTION—EVANGELISM. 65

The Gospel 65

Our Threefold Preparation 66

Go Make Disciples 69

Questions for Thought 71

EPILOGUE: 73

Our Legacy: What Really Matters? 73

Questions for Thought 76

ATTACHMENT 1. 77

God Is Transcendent 77

God Is Relational 79

ATTACHMENT 2. 83

Personality. 83

ATTACHMENT 3. 87

Aptitude Tests 87

ATTACHMENT 4. 89

Spiritual Gifts Testing 89

ABOUT THE AUTHORS 91

BIBLIOGRAPHY. 93

RESOURCES FOR ADDITIONAL STUDY 95

NOTES. 96

ACKNOWLEDGMENTS

Any book is the result of the efforts of many people. No author publishes their work in total isolation. We'd like to thank several people who came alongside us during the process and helped to bring polish to our rough efforts:

Dell Hyssong of the Hyssongs—former pastor and friend, Dell read one of the earliest versions of the book. His comments encouraged us to keep writing.

Wayne Hastings read and commented on an early version as well. His astute observations led to expansion of the topics and study questions to follow each chapter. He also suggested our audience was wider than we'd anticipated.

Judy Powell, good friend and prayer warrior, kept our efforts uplifted in prayer and convinced us our book had a wider focus than just personal use. Her comments convinced us to publish.

Jennifer Kopald, our first student for this text, asked the questions and gave us insight into what information we needed to make clearer or explain in more detail.

Derinda Babcock, cover artist and designer par excellence. She took our ideas of how the book should look and turned them into reality. Her formatting skill made the book much easier to read and made us look good!

ROY AND DEB HAGGERTY

Roy: I want to thank my wife, Deb, for being at my side as this book took form. Her Biblical knowledge, her God-given wisdom, and her advice and counsel appear on every page. Thank you, Deb, for co-authoring this book with me!

Deb: God has given Roy the ability to make complex subjects easy to understand. As he worked on concepts he felt needed to be understood by those seeking a deeper relationship with God, he found his simple outline expanding to book length. He is truly a man of wisdom and knowledge and has a deep love for God. I am blessed to be his wife.

And, of course, all honor, glory, and thanks go to our Lord and Savior, who was with us throughout the process, and without whom we would have had nothing to say.

INTRODUCTION

While I have learned a lot walking with God since he saved me over sixty years ago, my education continues. I have experienced God's love through many joyful and painful times, but I am only too cognizant of the fact I have so much farther to go.

Your spiritual journey, your love affair with God, is different from my own or Deb's. Everyone's spiritual journey is uniquely their own and unlike anyone else's. Only God knows where we are and where he will take us in our spiritual walk. Enjoy the journey God has planned for you.

God has given all of us the ability to know him and experience his love. God has given us the ability to love him if we so choose. And God has given us the Holy Spirit to help and guide us on our spiritual journey. The rest is up to us.

While we each have our own spiritual journeys, there are some truths that are relevant to all of us. As you read on, listen to and apply what God lays on your heart. To the extent anything in this book is of help to you, give God all the thanks and all the glory because the concept and the words could only have come from him.

—**Roy Haggerty**, Plymouth, Massachusetts, 2019

PROLOGUE

Experiencing God's Love in a Broken World—A Spiritual Journey is designed to encourage people who are Christians to know God more intimately and to serve him more effectively. What could be more awesome than being deeply in love with the One who created us for that very purpose?

This book provides the basis for study and discussion for one-on-one or small group mentoring. Our hope is you will take the time to meditate on these sections and discover what they mean to you. May the Holy Spirit guide you in your journey.

CHAPTER ONE

WHO DO WE SAY GOD IS?

OUR THEOLOGY:

Said simply, our theology is our view of God. Our view is based on our understanding of God's revelation of himself in the Bible and our spiritual journey. Our personal view of God exerts a great influence on us because we ultimately live our lives based on our belief (or lack thereof) about the existence and character of God.

Making this point many years ago, A.W. Tozer said, "What comes into our mind when we think of God is the most important thing about us."[1] Knowledge of God, his character and attributes, determines our worldview (what we think), how we act (our relationships with one another), and how we worship God (in spirit and truth).

How does God reveal himself to us? How can we know who he is and how he relates to us? What do we need to understand to appreciate who he is?

---

1 A.W. Tozer, *The Knowledge of the Holy* (New York: HarperCollins, 1961), 1.

GOD'S REVELATION OF HIMSELF IN CREATION

> The heavens declare the glory of God,
> and the sky above proclaims his handiwork.
> (Psalm 19:1)

> For the wrath of God is revealed from heaven against all ungodliness and unrighteousness of men, who by their unrighteousness suppress the truth. For what can be known about God is plain to them, because God has shown it to them. For his invisible attributes, namely, his eternal power and divine nature, have been clearly perceived, ever since the creation of the world, in the things that have been made. So they are without excuse. (Romans 1:18-20)

We know there is a God with eternal power and a divine nature by observing his creation. But knowing there is a God is not the same thing as knowing God. Through God's divine revelation in the Bible, we have the ability to know him.

GOD'S REVELATION OF HIMSELF THROUGH THE BIBLE.

Because we are a finite creation, we are limited in our ability to know and understand an infinite God. But the good news is our God has graciously revealed who he is in human terms we can understand. The Bible, having been inspired by God, gives us insight into his character and attributes. A partial list is in Attachment 1.

If we open our minds and hearts to him as we spend time with him in prayer, the more we learn about him in the Bible, the more we will grow in our understanding of who he is. As a result, our love for him will also grow. To the extent we know

God, as he reveals himself in the Bible, we develop our ability to put our faith and trust in him. Let's start with Psalm 111:

> Praise the LORD!
> I will give thanks to the LORD with my whole heart,
>   in the company of the upright, in the congregation.
> **Great** are the works of the LORD,
>   studied by all who delight in them.
> **Full of splendor and majesty** is his work,
>   and his **righteousness** endures forever.
> He has caused his **wondrous works** to be remembered;
>   the LORD is **gracious and merciful**.
> He provides food for those who fear him;
>   he **remembers his covenant** forever.
> He has shown his people the **power of his works,**
>   in giving them the inheritance of the nations.
> The works of his hands are **faithful and just**;
>   all his **precepts are trustworthy**;
> they are established forever and ever,
>   to be performed with faithfulness and uprightness.
> He sent redemption to his people;
>   he has commanded his covenant forever.
>   **Holy and awesome** is his name!
> The fear of the LORD is the beginning of wisdom;
>   all those who practice it have a good understanding.
> His praise endures forever! [bold is author's]

Great and wondrous are God's works. He is gracious and merciful as he keeps his covenant promises. All his precepts are trustworthy because he is faithful and just. Holy and awesome is his name (all that he is).

"The fear of the LORD is the beginning of wisdom" (v10). The Hebrew word we translate as *fear* in Psalm 111 does not mean to be afraid but to hold God in proper reverence and awe.

Two of God's attributes need our special attention. We live our lives in God's presence every second of the day (God is omnipresent or everywhere). God knows every thought, word, and action—every desire we have (God is omniscient or all-knowing). We need to be continuously mindful of these two truths. The more we know and love God, the more our awareness of the presence of God in our lives becomes a comfort to us as we face the trials and tribulations of life.

GOD'S REVELATION OF HIMSELF IN JESUS.

> And the Word became flesh and dwelt among us, and we have seen his glory, glory as of the only Son from the Father, full of grace and truth. (John 1:14)

We read about the incarnate Jesus in the gospels. We learn about who Jesus is, his earthly ministry, and how much he loves us.

The Bible gives us a visualization of Jesus as wholly God and as wholly man—a truth we cannot comprehend except by faith. Visualizing Jesus as wholly man becomes easier as we read the gospels that describe his life on earth. As to our desire to visualize Jesus as God, both the prophet Isaiah and the apostle John shared with us a vision they were given of Jesus as wholly God.

The preincarnate Jesus is described in the Book of Isaiah:

> In the year that King Uzziah died I saw the Lord sitting upon a throne, high and lifted up; and the train of his robe filled the temple. Above him stood the seraphim. Each had six wings: with two he covered his face, and with two he covered his feet, and with two he flew. And one called to another and said:

> "Holy, holy, holy is the LORD of hosts;
> the whole earth is full of his glory!"

> And the foundations of the thresholds shook at the voice of him who called, and the house was filled with smoke. And I said: "Woe is me! For I am lost; for I am a man of unclean lips, and I dwell in the midst of a people of unclean lips; for my eyes have seen the King, the LORD of hosts!" (Isaiah 6:1-5)

Repetition is the Hebrew language method of emphasis. The Trisagion, or triple use of the word "holy" indicates God's infinite holiness. This is Isaiah's vision of the preincarnate Jesus. "These things Isaiah said because he saw his glory, and he spoke of him" (John 12:41).

After his ascension, Jesus is described in the Book of Revelation:

> Then I saw heaven opened, and behold, a white horse! The one sitting on it is called Faithful and True, and in righteousness he judges and makes war. His eyes are like a flame of fire, and on his head are many diadems, and he has a name written that no one knows but himself. He is clothed in a robe dipped in blood, and the name by which he is called is The Word of God. And the armies of heaven, arrayed in fine linen, white and pure, were following him on white horses.
> From his mouth comes a sharp sword with which to strike down the nations, and he will rule them with a rod of iron. He will tread the winepress of the fury of the wrath of God the Almighty. On his robe and on his thigh he has a name written, King of kings and Lord of lords. (Revelation 19:11-16)

This description is filled with symbolism requiring an interpretation for anyone doing an exegetical study of Revelation. In Isaiah's vision, Jesus is described as "the King, the Lord of hosts." John's vision similarly describes Jesus as the "King of kings, Lord of lords."

QUESTIONS FOR THOUGHT

When was the last time you spent time focusing on and experiencing God's magnificent creation?_____

_____

_____

- Where were you?_____

_____

- What did you see?_____

_____

- Did you sense God's presence? His eternal power? His divine nature?_____

_____

_____

_____

We tend to be so busy with our daily activities, we do not take time to observe God's creation around us. Find a place you can be alone and let the Holy Spirit open your eyes to the beauty around you. Open your heart and let the Holy Spirit fill you with love, joy, and peace. (Gal. 5:22)

Go back and re-read Psalm 111 s-l-o-w-l-y. Meditate on the bold text that describes who God is and pray a prayer of joy and thanksgiving—that he loves you and you are his.

How does knowing God is present affect your relationship with God?_____

_____

_____

_____

An omnipresent God always, always is with us. What can you do to be aware of his presence throughout the day? Some people wear a cross around their necks. Some people carry a small Bible they can feel in their pocket or see in their purse. Some people put up notes with Scripture verses on their desks or walls. What can you do to keep God foremost in your thoughts?

_____

_____

_____

_____

_____

_____

We have been given a word picture of Jesus as both man and God during his earthly ministry. We also have a vision of Jesus as King of kings and Lord of lords as told to us through the prophet Isaiah and the apostle John. How do you think of Jesus as you go about your daily life? Do you talk with him? Is he a friend you go to for advice? Can you weep with him when you are sad? Rejoice with him during glad times? Write a conversational prayer telling him what place he has in your life.

_____

_____

_____

_____

_____

_____

_____

_____

_____

_____

_____

_____

_____

_____

_____

_____

_____

_____

_____

_____

_____

CHAPTER TWO
GOD'S RELATIONSHIP WITH US

WHAT DOES THE BIBLE TELL US?

Throughout history God has made two types of covenants with his people. The first type was a Royal Grant or an unconditional covenant:

The Noahic covenant (Genesis 9:8-17) was an unconditional divine promise to never again destroy all earthly life with some natural catastrophe, the covenant "sign" being the rainbow in a storm cloud.

The Abrahamic covenant (A) (Genesis 15:18-21) was an unconditional divine promise to fulfill the grant of the land.

The Phinehas covenant (Numbers 25:10-13) was an unconditional divine promise to maintain the family of Phinehas in a "perpetual priesthood" (implicitly a pledge to Israel to provide her forever with a faithful priesthood).

The Davidic covenant (2 Samuel 7:5-16) was an unconditional divine promise to establish and maintain the Davidic dynasty on the throne of Israel (implicitly a pledge to Israel) to provide her forever with a godly king like David and through that dynasty to do for her what he had done through David—bring her into rest in the promised land (1 Kings 4:20-21; 5:3-4).

God also made what was called a *suzerain-vassal* or a conditional covenant with his people:

The Abrahamic covenant (B) (Genesis 17) was a conditional divine pledge to be Abraham's God and the God of his descendants on the condition of total consecration to the Lord as symbolized by circumcision.

The Mosaic or Sinatic covenant (Exodus 19-24) was a conditional divine pledge to be Israel's God (as her Protector and the Guarantor of her blessed destiny) on the condition of Israel's total consecration to the Lord as His people who live by His rule and serve His purposes in history.[2]

God has been faithful, keeping all his covenant promises:

God has honored his Noahic covenant not to destroy all earthly life.

God fulfilled his Abrahamic covenant when Joshua entered the land that God had promised Abraham (Joshua 1:1-4).

We have, in Jesus, our great high priest forever fulfilling what is called the Phinehas covenant (Hebrews 4:14).

Jesus continues the kingly lineage of David (Matthew 1:1, 17).

God kept his covenant promise to Abraham and Moses to be their God provided they totally consecrated themselves to him. But throughout redemptive history, Israel rebelled and did not keep their covenant promises.

---

2. *Zondervzn NASB Study Bible*, "Major Covenants of the Old Testament," (Zondervan, 1999) 16

Time after time the Israelites did not honor their covenant with God by consecrating themselves to him, worshipping him alone, and keeping his commandments. Only when experiencing pain and suffering would they cry out to God, begging for mercy.

They would then promise to turn from their sinful ways and become faithful to God.

Most of us can identify with the Israelites. When we encounter a crisis in our life, or in the life of a loved one, be it a physical problem, an emotional problem, or a broken relationship, what do we do? We cry out to God. Our prayers become much longer and more intense. Once the crisis is resolved, whatever the outcome, we are tempted to take back control of our lives. It is like saying, 'Thank you Lord, I can take it from here." If this is your or my normal response, like the Israelites, we will have more difficulty dealing with the trials and tribulations of life.

Before continuing, we need to consider the impact of the New Covenant God made with Israel that now applies to us. The prophet Jeremiah prophesied that God would make a new unconditional covenant with Israel (Jeremiah 31:31-34). This new covenant is an unconditional divine promise to unfaithful Israel to forgive her sins and establish his relationship with her on a new basis by writing his law "on their heart"—a covenant of pure grace which is quoted in the eighth chapter of the Book to the Hebrews:

> But as it is, Christ has obtained a ministry that is as much more excellent than the old as the covenant he mediates is better, since it is enacted on better promises. For if that first covenant had been faultless, there would have been no occasion to look for a second.
> For he finds fault with them when he says:

"Behold, the days are coming, declares the Lord,
    when I will establish a new covenant with the
house of Israel
    and with the house of Judah,
not like the covenant that I made with their fathers
    on the day when I took them by the hand to
bring them out of the land of Egypt.
For they did not continue in my covenant,
    and so I showed no concern for them, declares
the Lord.
For this is the covenant that I will make with the
house of Israel
    after those days, declares the Lord:
I will put my laws into their minds,
    and write them on their hearts,
and I will be their God,
    and they shall be my people.
And they shall not teach, each one his neighbor
    and each one his brother, saying, 'Know the
Lord,'
for they shall all know me,
    from the least of them to the greatest.
For I will be merciful toward their iniquities,
    and I will remember their sins no more."

In speaking of a new covenant, he makes the first one obsolete. And what is becoming obsolete and growing old is ready to vanish away. (Hebrews 8:6-13)

The covenant Jeremiah prophesied is based on the forgiveness of sin.

The Law given to Moses was holy and good (Romans 7:12) but could not make sinful man righteous, nor provide the ability necessary to fulfill its demands (Hebrews 7:18-19a).

Unlike the Israelites living under the previous covenants, we, as Christians, are under the New Covenant. God has forgiven our sins and the Holy Spirit provides us the ability to live a holy life. Our problem is our fallen nature continues to battle the Holy Spirit for control.

It is not that we don't love God or are not thankful for his grace. It is not that we don't trust God or question that he is and will do what is best for us. It is not even that we believe our way is as good or better then God's way.

The reality is there are some aspects of our lives that we do not want to surrender to God's control, because in our minds, losing control violates the very essence of who we think we are. Embedded in our psyche is the notion of our need to achieve something—to do something. For the Christian, that need becomes a desire to do *good* works for God and for others.

In addition, our culture seems to demand we earn what we get, and as a result, we should get what we deserve. We have a strong desire to earn our way through life. We do not like to have anyone give us something for nothing. Consider the following:

- If someone invites you over to their house for dinner, do you feel obligated to invite them over to your house in return?
- If someone gives you a gift, do you think about its value and plan to give them an equivalent gift sometime later?
- If someone does you a favor, do you plan to balance the books by returning the favor?

When God gives us a gift or blesses us beyond what we can do for ourselves, what is our response? Our natural response is to want to contribute something to what God is doing in our lives.

Perhaps we can contribute our good works or our belief or our faith. If we can offer anything to God, we will have in some measure contributed. There is tremendous freedom and peace of mind when we are released from a works-righteousness mindset motivating our compliance to God's will. When we realize there is nothing we can do to receive God's grace, we are free to simply respond to God's love and grace by loving God with all our heart, soul, mind, and strength. Our love for God becomes the motivation for us to surrender our will to God's will and enjoy a loving relationship forever with him.

QUESTIONS FOR THOUGHT

What do all of God's covenants tell us about him? _____

_____

_____

_____

_____

_____

- Is God trustworthy? If you answer yes, why is this important to you?_____

_____

_____

_____

_____

_____

- Does God provide the Israelites with second chances? Does he do the same with us? How do you know? Give examples.

_____

_____

_____

_____

_____

• Has God throughout redemptive history responded to the prayers of his people? How does this truth impact your desire to pray?_____

_____

_____

_____

_____

• What else can we learn from reading God's covenants?

_____

_____

_____

_____

As Christians, we live under the new covenant of grace and the power of the Holy Spirit. What would your life be like if you were to live each day releasing control of your thoughts, words, and actions to the Holy Spirit? Think of specific examples of how you would be changed. Is this the desire of your heart?

_____

_____

_____

_____

_____

_____

CHAPTER THREE

OUR PERSONAL RELATIONSHIP WITH GOD

Do we, personally, have a loving relationship with God?

The word "love" as commonly used by us is so broad in its meaning that love means what ever a person wants the word to mean. Our English dictionary provides twenty-eight definitions and forty-seven synonyms—not at all surprising. For example:

I love my wife, I love pizza, I love fast cars, I love the Red Sox.

When your wife enters a room with a new outfit on and asks, "What do you think?" You may get by with "I like it." But you get a different reaction if you say "I love it!"

If your wife asks you what your opinion is of some other woman and you say "I love her," you better have a common understanding of what you meant by "love."

Classical Greek, unlike English, uses different words to describe what we call "love." The two Greek words translated into English as the word "love" that concern us in Bible translations are *agapē* and *phileō*.

This [agapē] is one of the least frequent words in classical Greek, where it expresses, on the few occasions it occurs, that highest and noblest form of love which sees something infinitely precious in its object … It [phileō] is more naturally used of intimate affection[3].

Jesus used both agapē and phileō when he was asked by one of the scribes to answer a question that was being debated at the time:

> "Which commandment is the most important of all?"
>
> Jesus answered, "The most important is, 'Hear, O Israel: The Lord our God, the Lord is one. And you shall love [agapē] the Lord your God with all your heart and with all your soul and with all your mind and with all your strength.' The second is this: You shall love [phileō] your neighbor as yourself.' There is no other commandment greater than these."(Mark 12:28b-31)

We aspire to love God with the highest and noblest form of love. Although we can never attain that goal, do our actions more and more reflect the agapē form of love?

Christians live under the New Covenant and have, as a result, direct access to God. At some point in our lives, each of us has heard the gospel, and God ["having the eyes of your hearts enlightened" (Ephesians 1:18a)] gave us the ability to understand and believe what the gospel tells us is true. When we believed the gospel of Jesus Christ, we repented of our sins. Repentance is not only turning away from our sin but also includes turning to Jesus. Having believed the gospel and repented of our sins, we acknowledged Jesus as our Lord and Savior and accepted God's gift of salvation. We then began our relationship with our God.

---

3 *New Bible Dictionary*, Second Edition, (Tyndale, 1962), p. 711

There's a story about a man and a woman. One day, the man tells the woman he loves her with all his heart and asks her to marry him. He wants her to be his bride. She excitedly says "Yes!" But then she says, "However, there are certain conditions that must be understood. I don't plan to spend a lot of time with you, and I plan to continue my current lifestyle doing whatever I want." The boy loves the girl so much that he agrees to her conditions hoping over time she will learn to love him more and will want to spend more time with him.

The story about the man and the woman has a happy ending. Soon after they were married, the woman begins to spend more and more time with the man and misses him when she is not with him. Their relationship becomes a true love affair that grows throughout their life on earth and is perfected when they reach heaven. Our relationship with God can also grow and have a happy ending.

We need to ask ourselves if any part of the story reflects our relationship with God. How much time do we spend with God? How much have we changed from before we were saved? Do we live our lives striving to love God with all our heart, soul, mind, and strength (ability)?

I have noticed many people who regularly attend churches on Sundays seem to have fallen in love with the *idea* of God (based on their understanding of God) but have not yet experienced the joy of falling in love *with* God. Falling in love with the idea of God can be a step in the right direction and has the potential to inspire the desire to have a more intimate, loving relationship with God. God is willing. The question is—are we willing?

How could we describe a loving relationship with God? Steve Brown of Key Life Ministries makes an interesting observation, "There is something about being loved unconditionally, forgiven totally, and accepted without reservation by God that solicits laughter."[4]

Do we experience joy and laughter while having a good time with God, or do we only, on occasion, solemnly bow our heads in prayer trying to find the "right" words? Does spending time alone with God by reading his Word and talking to him in prayer seem like a chore to get through? Do we spend our time with God making our concerns and requests known and then run out of things to say? Our relationship shouldn't be that way! Our time with God should be filled with joy and laughter in addition to voicing our concerns and requests. I think Steve Brown seems to be saying, "Lighten-up and enjoy a loving relationship with your God."

Bill Myers's book *The Jesus Experience* provides some insight into his spiritual journey and gives us good advice as to what we can do to build our loving relationship with God. The following is what I believe Bill is telling us:

---

4 Steve Brown, "Perverting God," *Key Life Newsletter*, June, 2018.

First, we need to be still and listen to God speak to us as we read his Word.

Second, we need to spend time talking to God through our prayers. The prayer Jesus gave us begins "Our Father." These two words can also be translated as "Our Daddy," "Our Papa," "Our Dad." These terms of endearment are those a loving child would use to his Father.[5]

The more we are mindful of God's presence during our day, the more we see God's blessings in our daily lives. However, we also begin to see the extent of our sin. If we are not careful, we can become ashamed, frustrated, and begin to have a negative view of ourselves and as a result, we tend to want to hide from God like Adam and Eve did when they had disobeyed.

Remember, God has always seen who we are and what we have done. We, not God, are the ones becoming more and more aware of our sinfulness. The good news is an all-knowing God has forgiven our sins and loves us exactly the way we are. There is nothing we have done or will ever do that God does not know, yet God totally and unconditionally loves us.

We need to remember that having a loving relationship with our Creator is not restrictive—our relationship is liberating when we realize we can and do indeed have joy, fun, and laughter when we spend time with him.

We experience becoming a new creation at the time of our salvation, and therefore, our salvation should be the beginning of a wonderful love affair with our Heavenly Father.

---

5 Bill Myers, *The Jesus Experience*, (Shiloh Run Press, 2015), pp.49-57

The more we know him and experience his love, the more we will love him. Over time, our love of God will change us, and this change will be obvious to everyone who knows us.

QUESTIONS FOR THOUGHT

Give examples of how you most often use the word *love*.

_____

_____

_____

_____

What is the difference between the Greek words agapē and phileō? _____

_____

_____

How would you describe your one-on-one time with your heavenly Father? _____

_____

_____

_____

Write some examples of when your time with God resulted in joy and laughter._____

_____

_____

_____

_____

Bill Myers has given us insight into his spiritual journey. What more can you do to enhance and expand your spiritual journey?

_____

_____

_____

_____

God knows the impact our fallen nature and Satan have on our ability to love him with an agapē love. He also knows, and so should we, that we will be able to love him free from any constraints when we get to heaven. Until then, we pray the Holy Spirit will help us grow more and more in love with our God.

CHAPTER FOUR
WHO ARE WE?

WHO DO WE SAY WE ARE?

Mark Batterson in *Soulprint* frames the answer well: "Most of us live our entire lives as strangers to ourselves. We know more about others than we know about ourselves. Our true identities get buried beneath the mistakes we've made, the insecurities we've acquired, and the lies we've believed. We're held captive by others' expectations. We're uncomfortable in our own skin. And we spend far too much emotional, relational, and spiritual energy trying to be who we're not."[6]

In other words, we tend to live with a defensive posture of being who other people want/expect us to be. Why do we care what other people think about us? The reason is we all desire to be liked, respected, and we hope, loved.

Unfortunately, we live in an environment that is spiritually toxic. The people who live in this world, including us, fall short of God's righeousness, his standards, because of sin. Other people's

---

6 Mark Batterson, *Soulprint*, (Multinomah Books, 2015), 3.

input, even well-intentioned people, should not be the basis of our view of self-worth.

From the first day of our lives, the environment in which we live and the people with whom we share our world have been wielding a strong influence on our perceptions of ourselves. Just think about the following questions:

- What names were you called growing up? How did they affect you?

- What positive and negative influences did parents and teachers have on your view of yourself?

- Do you tend to still remember the criticism you have received in your life, or do you remember the past compliments?

Some of us are still trying to figure out who we really are. We often represent who we are differently depending on where we are and who we are with. We continue to evaluate our self-worth based on who others think we are.

Is this behavior normal—yes! But before further discussion of who we are and how we think and act, we need to discuss God's sovereignty and man's freedom to act as a moral agent—a person who has the ability to discern right from wrong and to be held accountible for their own actions.

GOD'S SOVEREIGNTY AND MAN'S FREE WILL

Simply stated, God's sovereignty means he is in total control of everything that happens in his creation, including what happens by us and to us. Nothing happens outside the will of God.

> But Joseph said to them, "Do not fear, for am I in the place of God? As for you, you meant evil against me, but God meant it for good, to bring it about that many people should be kept alive, as they are today. (Genesis 50:19-20)

> The heart of man plans his way, but the Lord establishes his steps. (Proverbs 19:9)

> In him we have obtained an inheritance, having been predestined according to the purpose of him who works all things according to the counsel of his will. (Ephesians 1:11)

On the other hand, our freedom of the will is generally believed to mean we can make decisions and take responsibility for our actions.

> And if it is evil in your eyes to serve the LORD, choose this day whom you will serve. (Joshua 14:15a)

> Therefore, I will judge you, O house of Israel, everyone according to his ways, declares the Lord God. Repent and turn from all your transgressions, lest iniquity be your ruin. (Ezekiel 18:30)

> For you were called to freedom, brothers. Only do not use your freedom as an opportunity for the flesh, but through love serve one another. (Galatians 15:13)

Whatever definitions we choose for God's sovereignty and man's free will, the Bible appears to leave us with a contradiction. Is God in control of man's decisions and actions, or does man decide and act on his own without any outside interference? We hate unresolved contradictions, so what do we do?

What we need to consider is that this contradiction is an *antinomy*. An antinomy is an apparent contradiction between conclusions which seem equally logical, reasonable or necessary. We must be open to the Bible's assurance that God's sovereignty and man's free will are both true.

We should not be surprised by the appearance of mysteries like this in God's Word.

> Oh, how great are God's riches and wisdom and knowledge! How impossible it is for us to understand his decisions and his ways! (Romans 11:33 NLT)

Therefore, we must be careful not to affirm God's sovereignty in a way that releases man of his responsibilities. Likewise, we must be careful not to limit God's sovereignty by stating man's free will exists outside God's sovereignty.

Perhaps it is helpful to think of God's sovereignty as having two components—one his *efficacious* will and the other his *permissive* will. Efficacious means producing or capable of producing a desired or intended result. God's efficacious will directly produces the fulfillment of his desires. His permissive will indirectly fulfills his desires. God, being sovereign, *permits* man to have free will—an expression of his permissive will. If God had not given man free will and permission to exercise it, we would not have the ability to make decisions based on our own understanding and desires.

With free will comes responsibility and accountability. As Christians, we should always seek to know what God wants us to do and align our God-granted free will with what God desires of us.

UNDERSTANDING FREE WILL

For hundreds of years, philosophers and theologians have had only a few areas of agreement. But one of the important areas of general agreement is how and why man makes decisions. The following is from a seminary paper I wrote in 1990 on Jonathan Edwards's contribution regarding man's "free will."

> In summary, the Will is the faculty of choice. The acts of the Will such as refusing, approving, rejecting, and determining are all acts of choosing. In order for there to be an act of choosing there must be a motive. The Will does not make a choice without a reason, the Will always follows the last dictate of understanding of that which is most good and pleasing to the mind. Therefore, there must be, in an absolute and certain sense, a necessary connection between motive and choice.

> Freedom or liberty is the power, opportunity, or advantage, to do as one pleases. This "freedom" must be free from constraint such as force, compulsion, coaction, or not having the power of choice.

> There is also agreement that if we make choices strictly from a neutral posture, with no prior inclination, then we make choices for no reason. In fact, we would make no choice at all. Even if we suppose one could make a choice for no reason, there is no moral significance and the choice, therefore, can not be judged good or bad. God is concerned about our motives; if we could make a choice for no reason there is no motive.

> However, freedom of the Will as we have observed is the ability to make choices according to our desires. This means that the Will always chooses according to its strongest inclination at that moment. These

inclinations are produced by the connection of secondary causes. That is, inclinations are produced by something that previously or currently exists; every inclination has a cause. This means every choice is "free" and, in a sense, every choice is determined.[7]

The big idea is we make decisions based on what we *perceive* to be most good and pleasing to our mind at the point when a decision is made. In other words, what we perceive is in our self-interest. This *perception* is based on motives we have because of previous thoughts and/or experiences.

We humans are wired to make decisions based on perceptions as to what is good for us that unfortunately are corrupted by our fallen nature. The apostle Paul described this condition in what is referred to as his "wretched man" comments:

> For the good that I want, I do not do, but I practice the very evil that I do not want. I am no longer the one doing it, but sin which dwells in me. I find then the principle that evil is present in me, the one who wants to do good, for I joyfully concur with the law of God in the inner man, but I see a different law in the members of my body, waging war against the law of my mind and making me a prisoner of the law of sin which is in my members. Wretched man that I am! Who will set me free from the body of this death? (Romans 7:19-24)

I have heard many Christians use these verses to justify in their own minds their sinful thoughts, words, and actions. They say, "After all, even the apostle Paul could not control his sinful nature corrupting his God-wired decision-making process. Therefore, what chance do I have?"

---

7 Roy Haggerty, "Edwards on Free Will, " 1990, p.11

Setting aside the problem of using another human being as the standard for ourselves, is Paul voicing frustration regarding his inability to not sin? Yes, and what Paul is also saying is the Law gives us knowledge of sin and confronts us with the reality we are sinners: There is none righteous, not even one; ... because by the works of the Law no flesh will be justified in His sight; for through the Law comes the knowledge of sin. (Romans 3:10, 20)

The good news is the book to the Romans does not end with chapter 7 and mankind marred in sin with no ability to avoid God's judgment for our transgressions.

Christians, who have by God's grace through faith repented of their sins and accepted Jesus as their Lord and Savior, are forgiven for their sins because of Jesus's atoning sacrifice on the cross. At the instant of our salvation, our gracious God has forgiven our sins and sealed our adoption into his family and eternal life with him in heaven.

But what about our remaining time on earth? We still have a fallen nature. We still are "wired" the same way to make decisions. We still must contend with the devil's attacks. Good news! God does not leave us without any hope. After Paul describes himself (and by extension, us) as "a wretched man" in chapter 7 of Romans based on what the Law tells him (us), he then introduces the work of the Holy Spirit in chapter 8. God has provided us with the indwelling Holy Spirit to help us.

J. I. Packer in his book, *Keep in Step with the Spirit*, describes the ministry of the Holy Spirit:

> The distinctive, constant, basic ministry of the Holy Spirit under the new covenant is to mediate Christ's presence to believers–that is, to give them such

knowledge of his presence with them as their Savior, Lord, and God—that three things keep happening: First, personal fellowship with Jesus ... Second, personal transformation of character into Jesus' likeness ... and Third, the Spirit-given certainty of being loved, redeemed, and adopted through Christ into the Father's family ...

The gospel, says Paul, is a summons to "... be renewed in the spirit of your minds, and put on the new nature, created after the likeness of God in true righteousness and holiness" (Ephesians 4:23-24). The born-again believer, who is in good spiritual health, aims each day at perfect obedience, perfect righteousness, perfect pleasing of his heavenly Father; it is his nature to do so. Does he ever achieve it? Not in this world. In this respect he cannot do what he would.[8]

Our spiritual growth—becoming more and more like Christ—is a process (not a one-time event like our salvation) that is aided by the Holy Spirit. This is where our free will comes into play. We must cooperate with the Holy Spirit if we are to have spiritual growth—the process of sanctification.

We have said free will is the ability to make decisions based on what is most good and pleasing to our mind when a decision is made. Prior to becoming a Christian, our fallen nature determined what we believed to be in our self-interest, but now, we have a new nature that gives us the desire to do what is pleasing to God.

As our love of God grows, what is good and pleasing to the mind becomes more and more what our hearts tell us is pleasing

---

8 J. I. Packer, (*Keep in Step with the Spirit*, Revell, 1984), p. 49, 110

to God, which determines the decisions we make. With the help of the Holy Spirit, we can begin the process of undoing all the misconceptions and hurt we have accumulated over our lives—those things that drag us down and lead to sinful decisions and provide the devil a way to attack us.

We need to begin anew by removing the garbage we have stored in our minds prior to our being born-again. This process is not for the faint of heart. We will continue to have many failures along the way. But God still loves us totally, unconditionally, and knows the struggles we face.

Who are you? Who am I? Unlike the rest of creation, we are made in God's image with intellect, emotions, and a will. God loves us and gave us the ability to love him. We should not wait until we are in heaven. During our time on earth, we can enjoy a loving relationship with our Creator; we can become more and more Christ-like every day; and we can serve our God using all the capabilities and spiritual gifts God has given us for that purpose.

Questions for Thought

List the people who have had the most influence on how you feel about yourself. _____

_____

_____

_____

_____

Why did they have such a profound effect on you? _____

_____

_____

_____

_____

In your own words, define "free will" and God's "sovereignty."

_____

_____

_____

_____

_____

Is asking God to change you to be more Christlike an act of free will? Explain. _____

_____

_____

_____

_____

When the Holy Spirit helps us become more Christlike, is this an act of God's sovereignty? Explain. _____

_____

_____

_____

_____

How have you changed since becoming a Christian? _____

_____

_____

_____

_____

_____

_____

The more the desires of our heart are to love God and walk with him, the more the Holy Spirit is able to change us from our old selves to become the person God wants us to be. One important step in this process is to see ourselves as God sees us.

CHAPTER FIVE

WHO DOES GOD SAY WE ARE?

You *may* be as surprised as I was by how often and in how many ways Scripture describes who God says you and I are:

> I am the salt of the earth. (Matt 5:13)
>
> I am the light of the world. (Matt 5:14)
>
> I am a child of God, part of His family. (John 1:12; Rom 8:16)
>
> I am part of the true vine, a channel of Christ's life. (John 15:12, 5)
>
> I am Christ's friend. (John 15:15)
>
> I am chosen and appointed by Christ to bear His fruit. (John 15:16)
>
> I am a son of God. God is spiritually my Father. (Rom 8:14-15; Gal 3:26, 4:6)
>
> I am no longer under condemnation, because I am in Christ. (Rom 8:1)
>
> I am joint heir with Christ, sharing His inheritance with Him. (Rom 8:17)
>
> I am accepted by Christ, sharing His inheritance with Him. (Rom 8:17)
>
> I am accepted by Christ and belong in His family. (Rom 15:7; Eph 1:6)
>
> I am sanctified, set apart for His use. (1 Cor 1:2)
>
> I am a temple (home) of God. His Spirit (His life) dwells in me. (1 Cor 3:16; 6:19)

I am a member (part) of Christ's body. (1 Cor 12:27; Eph 5:30)

I am a new creation in Christ. (2 Cor 12:27; Eph 5:30)

I am reconciled to God and am an ambassador for Christ. (2 Cor 5:18-20)

I am the righteousness of God because of Christ. (2 Cor 5:21)

I am a son of God and one with other believers in Christ. (Gal 3:26, 28)

I am an heir of God since I am a son of God. (Gal 4:6-7)

I am a saint. (1 Cor 1:2; Eph 1:1; Phil 1:1; Col 1:2)

I am blessed with every spiritual blessing. (Eph 1:3)

I am chosen, holy and blameless before God. (Eph 1:4)

I am secure and sealed by the power of the Holy Spirit. (2 Cor 1:22)

I am God's workmanship (handiwork) created (born anew) in Christ to do His work that he planned beforehand that I should do. (Eph 2:10)

I am a fellow citizen with the rest of God's people in His family. (Eph 2:19)

I am righteous and holy. (Eph 4:24)

I am a citizen of heaven and seated in heaven right now. (Eph 2:6; Phil 3:20)

I am hidden with Christ in God. (Col 3:3)

I am an expression of the life of Christ because he is my life. (Col 3:4)

I am chosen of God, holy, and dearly loved. (Col 3:12)

I am a son of light and not of darkness. (1 Thess 5:5)

I am a partaker of Christ, and I share in His life. (Heb 3:14)

I am one of God's living stones being built up (in Christ) as a spiritual house. (1 Pet 2:5)I am a chosen race, a royal priesthood, a holy nation, a people for

God's own possession to proclaim His praises. (1 Pet 2:9-10)

I am an alien and stranger to this world I temporarily live in. (1 Pet 2:11)

I am an enemy of the devil. (1 Pet 5:8)

I am a child of God. When Christ returns, I will be like Him. (1 John 3:1-2)

I am born of God and the evil one (the devil) cannot touch me. (1 John 5:18)[9]

The writers of the New Testament, under the inspiration of the Holy Spirit, continually remind us who God says we are in Christ. If we are honest with ourselves, we will admit we need to be constantly reminded of this truth and know that his opinion is the only one that matters.

God has blessed us with a new life in Christ. He has blessed us with the Holy Spirit to guide and aid us in our spiritual growth. And he has blessed us with the gift of a free will, so we can choose to love him as our personal act of worship.

What Is Our Response?

Before answering this critical question, we need to look at history. We read in the Old Testament that God gave the nation of Israel laws and practices to live by. The Pharisees equated righteous living with law-keeping. To instruct people as to what they believed God's laws said, they added clarification to his laws

---

9 Adapted from Neil Anderson, *Living Free in Christ* (Bethany Books, Bloomington, MN 2001)

resulting in 613 rabbinical laws: 248 that were positive, and 365 that were negative.

In the New Testament, by one person's count, there are 147 principles and directives Jesus gave us to live by. Should we consider all 147 of equal importance? In one sense, the answer is yes. To disregard or ignore the principles and directives Jesus gave us is sin and any sin, no matter how minor we think it is, is a sin against an infinitely holy God and, therefore, should be considered infinitely bad.

As important as the whole counsel of God is for us to live by, the subject of *Experiencing God's Love in a Broken World* requires we pay special attention to Jesus's answer to the question asked by one of the scribes (teachers of the Law) about which commandment is the most important of all.

Jesus answered by quoting not one but two Old Testament commandments. The first was Deuteronomy 6:4-5 (the Shema—the Jewish statement of faith), the second was Leviticus 19:18b.

> "Which commandment is the most important of all?" Jesus answered, "The most important is, 'Hear, O Israel: The Lord our God, the Lord is one. And you shall love the Lord your God with all your heart and with all your soul and with all your mind and with all your strength.' The second is this: 'You shall love your neighbor as yourself.' There is no other commandment greater than these" (Mark 12:28b-31).

Why are these two commandments of such great importance? In the book of Samuel, we read this verse: "But the LORD said to Samuel, 'Do not look on his appearance or on the height of his stature, because I have rejected him. For the LORD sees not as man sees, man looks at the outward appearance, but the LORD looks at the heart'" (1 Samuel 16:7).

God looks at what motivates all our actions. If our actions flow from our love (*agapē*) for him, we will be motivated to love (*phileō*) our neighbors. God is pleased when our actions are motivated out of our love for him!

Jesus said, "If you love me, you will keep my commandments" (John 14:15). Jesus is not telling us to prove our love. What he is saying is when we love him more than we love sin, we will be motivated by our love for him to keep his commandments—we are wired to do so voluntarily and with great joy.

Loving God is the first and foremost commandment not in order of importance, but because loving God is the reason that enables us to keep all the other commandments starting with our love for others.

QUESTIONS FOR THOUGHT

Read the verses describing who God says we are again. Pick out the verses that are most meaningful to you.

_____

_____

_____

_____

As you spend time reading your Bible, notice the verses where God says who you are. At different times in your spiritual walk, the number of verses most meaningful to you will increase.

Why did Jesus tell us loving God and our neighbors are the most important commandments? _____

_____

_____

_____

Can you list the Ten Commandments?

1._____

2._____

3._____

4._____

5._____

6._____

7._____

8._____

9._____

10._____

How much easier is following these commandments when you love God and your neighbors? _____

_____

_____

_____

Why? _____

_____

_____

_____

In what ways does your life demonstrate your love for others?

_____

_____

_____

_____

CHAPTER SIX

HOW DO WE CONNECT WITH GOD?

We have learned who God is and who God says we are. What a wonderful relationship we can have. But how do we approach him? How do we "connect" with our Father? What is the role of the Holy Spirit in helping us connect with the Father?

There are three major ways we, the created, have fellowship with God, the creator: Prayer, Worship, and the ministry of the Holy Spirit.

PRAYER:

Philippians 4:4-7 gives us some guidance The verses tell us the attitude we should have, what we should do, and one of the benefits of our prayers.

> Rejoice in the Lord always; again I will say rejoice. Let your reasonableness be known to everyone. The Lord is at hand; do not be anxious about anything, but in everything by prayer and supplication with thanksgiving let your requests be made known to God. And the peace of God, which passes all understanding, will guard your hearts and your minds in Christ Jesus.

We are told to always rejoice. In James 1: 2-4, we are told to "count it all joy, my brothers, when you meet trials of various kinds, for you know that the testing of your faith produces steadfastness. And let steadfastness have its perfect effect, that you may be perfect and complete, lacking in nothing."

We are told to be known as "reasonable" people. The New American Standard Version says "let your gentle *spirit* be known to all men." The King James Version says "let your moderation be known to all men." So we are to be humble before God and others, gentle in spirit, knowing who God is and who we are to him.

An acronym often used to help us remember what we should include in our prayers is ACTS:

- **A**doration: We are to bow in adoration and praise before our awesome God in reverence for who God is.

- **C**onfession: We are to confess our sins and transgressions in realization of who we are as flawed humanity.

- **T**hanksgiving: We are to thank him for the many blessings he bestows on us and the grace for living he gives us anew every morning.

- **S**upplication: We are to ask him for our needs and desires.

The root word in Greek for supplication, *deésis*, indicates a felt need that is *personal* and *urgent* or arising out of a personal need. So we are to pray for our needs but always with a spirit of thankfulness. And then we will have peace—the peace from God that surpasses our ability to understand.

There is no specific "right" time for prayers—no right length. A prayer can be a quiet whisper in a moment of need or a longer prayer listing all our needs and perhaps including intercession for others. Some people pray constantly, talking to God throughout their day. Others have specific times and places where they study his Word and pray. The point is prayer brings us closer to God and lets him demonstrate his love for us by listening to the pleas of his children. Prayer is one of the ways we can experience God's presence and love.

WORSHIP:

Scripture tells us much about worship. Music is often a way we worship. Music should be adoration and prayer wrapped in melody. Rather than just getting emotionally tied up with the beat and the chords, we should be able to hear the words and use them to reflect our worship of God.

John 4:24 tells us "God is spirit, and those who worship him must worship in spirit and in truth." In Psalm 96:9, we are told to "worship the LORD in the splendor of holiness; tremble before him, all the earth!" Just prior to verse 9, the Psalmist says "ascribe to the LORD the glory due his name."

Worship in the Hebrew comes from the verb *hitpael*, which means to bow down or prostrate oneself before a superior in homage. In Greek, the word is *sebó*—to reverence, worship, adore—show reverence or awe.

So what is worship? Worship is praise to God with a deep reverence and sense of awe. To praise him for who he is and what he has done throughout history and for us. Worship should be constant, whenever we think about him—before we pray, after we pray. That sense of awe should permeate our being. When we worship him through music, we should be experiencing that awe. What a privilege to have a relationship with God Most High and the opportunity to worship him!

MINISTRY OF THE HOLY SPIRIT:

Romans 8:26-27 gives us one of the roles of the Holy Spirit succinctly. "Likewise the Spirit helps us in our weakness. For we do not know what to pray for as we ought, but the Spirit himself intercedes for us with groanings too deep for words. And he who searches hearts knows what is the mind of the Spirit, because the Spirit intercedes for the saints according to the will of God."

In John 16:8-11, 13, Jesus tells us:

> And when he [the Holy Spirit] comes, he will convict the world concerning sin and righteousness and judgment: concerning sin, because they do not believe in me; concerning righteousness, because I go to the Father, and you will see me no longer; concerning judgment, because the ruler of this world is judged. ... When the Spirit of truth comes, he will guide you into all the truth, for he will not speak on his own authority, but whatever he hears he will speak, and he will declare to you the things that are to come.

The Holy Spirit does the will of God the Father and Jesus on earth, and his ministry is to be with us—to prompt us to do God's will, to prod us when we do wrong or are about to do wrong, and to provide comfort to us when we are in doubt or afraid. God is with us in the Person of the Holy Spirit as we live our daily lives. We can be relieved knowing when we pray to our heavenly Father, if we're don't know what to say, the Spirit will intercede and communicate what is in our hearts to him.

What an intimate relationship! God with us and in us always—available to guide, to reproach, and to reassure us on a moment by moment basis. Indeed, we *can* count it all joy even when we suffer trials knowing God created us, God loves and saved us, and God is with us always.

QUESTIONS FOR THOUGHT

What if anything should we do to prepare before we come before the Lord in prayer? _____

_____

_____

_____

_____

_____

What does worship mean to you? _____

_____

_____

_____

_____

Where do you enjoy worshipping God the most and why?

_____

_____

_____

_____

What are the primary ministries of the Holy Spirit in our prayer, worship of the Father, and our daily lives?

_____

_____

_____

_____

_____

_____

_____

What can you do to enhance your times of prayer and worship?

_____

_____

_____

_____

_____

_____

_____

_____

CHAPTER SEVEN

WHY ARE WE HERE?

WHAT IS OUR PURPOSE?

The *Westminster Shorter Catechism,* in response to the first question of the catechism, "What is the chief end of man?" provides the answer, "Man's chief end is to glorify God and to enjoy him forever."[1] The question and answer are based on the following three Scriptures:

> So, whether you eat or drink, or whatever you do, do all to the glory of God. (1 Corinthians 10:31)

> For from him and through him and to him are all things. To him be glory forever. Amen. (Romans 11:36)

> Whom have I in heaven but you? And there is nothing on earth that I desire besides you. (Psalm 73:25)

When we truly love God, we will first and foremost glorify him through praise and worship and enjoy our love affair with him.

---

1 *Westminster Shorter Catechism*, (Free Presbyterian Publications, 1985), p. 287

And in addition, over time, our love for God will become more and more the dominant influence of our thoughts, words, and actions.

Is there something God wants each of us to do?

God has a plan for our lives and a specific assignment he has prepared for us to complete.

God spoke through the prophet Jeremiah to the Israelites, who were in Babylon in exile from Jerusalem:

> For I know the plans I have for you, declares the LORD, plans for welfare and not for evil, to give you a future and a hope. (Jeremiah 29:11)

The apostle Paul in his letter to the Ephesians wrote:

> But God, being rich in mercy, because of the great love with which he loved us, even when we were dead in our trespasses, made us alive together with Christ—by grace you have been saved—and raised us up with him and seated us with him in the heavenly places in Christ Jesus, so that in the coming ages he might show the immeasurable riches of his grace in kindness toward us in Christ Jesus. For by grace you have been saved through faith. And this is not your own doing; it is the gift of God, not a result of works, so that no one may boast. (Ephesians 2:4-9)

Because of our union with Christ, God, our Father, has adopted us and given us a seat at the table with Jesus, our Lord and Savior, as a member of his family. We can look forward to riches beyond our comprehension in heaven as a result of our salvation. Although the Bible doesn't tell us, we may ask why we are still stumbling around here on earth constantly battling (and often failing) to overcome our fallen nature and the devil instead of going directly to heaven the moment we are saved. One possible answer may be found in the next verse:

> For we are his workmanship, created in Christ Jesus
> for good works, which God prepared beforehand, that
> we should walk in them. (Ephesians 2:10)

This verse indicates God has tasks for us to accomplish based on his sovereign plan and purpose. As has been said by others, if we are alive there is more God wants us to do.

This brings us to a second question. How are we to prepare to be able to perform the good works God has planned for us? What is most important is we must be willing to do what God says is required. God, after listing some of what he had done for his people, tells the Israelites through the prophet Micah what he wants them to do:

> O people, the LORD has told you what is good, and
> this is what he requires of you: to do what is right,
> to love mercy, and to walk humbly with your God.
> (Micah 6:8 NLT)

We are to transform our lives to God's will. First, we are to "do what is right." The Bible gives us an understanding of what is righteousness and what is sin. When we study Scripture, we are constantly reminded what is right in the eyes of God and made aware of the areas of our life where we still fall short.

Second, we are to love mercy. If we love mercy, we will have a heart filled with compassion for other people and their needs.

Last, we are to walk humbly with God. We are to live our lives in the presence of God humbling ourselves before him. When we walk with God, we do not try to run ahead of him to solve our problems ourselves or fall behind him by procrastinating about taking the action he wants us to do.

In order to become the person God wants us to be, we need to develop the capabilities God has given us—we need to identify what natural abilities we have, we need to determine what additional abilities we have an aptitude to learn, we need to identify what our spiritual gifts are, and we need to discover what desires for service God has laid on our hearts.

After we have listened to God speak to us through the desires of our heart, he will open our eyes to see opportunities to minister to others. These opportunities will give us the joy of having God minister through us in a very practical way.

> "You are the light of the world. A city set on a hill cannot be hidden. Nor do people light a lamp and put it under a basket, but on a stand, and it gives light to all in the house. In the same way, **let your light shine before others, so that they may see your good works and give glory to your Father who is in heaven.**"(Matthew 5:14-16, emphasis author's)

We are to let Jesus's light shine through us and manifest itself in our good deeds. But, if we stop there, everyone will praise *us* for the good things *we* do. Therefore, we must also let people know the source of our motivation to do good deeds, so everyone will praise our heavenly Father.

HOW DO WE DISCOVER OUR ASSIGNMENTS FROM GOD?

Before we look around for something to do for God, we must look within ourselves. God has uniquely created each of us with the ability to complete our God-given assignments:

First, we need to understand the personality God has given us. Webster's defines personality as the complex of characteristics that distinguishes a particular individual. Hippocrates was perhaps the first to attempt to describe these traits. Since then, hundreds of methods have been developed to determine our personality or temperament. One of the most well known is the Myers-Briggs assessment, which measures sixteen ways in which we see the world and make decisions. A simpler method was developed by Fred and Florence Littauer, now called "Wired that Way Personality Profile." (Attachment 2)

Second, we need to identify what abilities and aptitudes God has given us. We all have abilities and aptitudes we have not discovered yet. Aptitude tests are used to determine our ability/ potential to succeed in a certain task, with no prior knowledge or training. There are thousands to choose from. Several are listed in Attachment 3.

Third, we need to identify our spiritual gifts.

> Now there are varieties of gifts, but the same Spirit; and there are varieties of service, but the same Lord; and there are varieties of activities, but it is the same God who empowers them all in everyone. To each is given the manifestation of the Spirit for the common good. (1 Cor 12:4–7)

See Attachment 4 for spiritual gifts assessments.

Fourth, and most revealing, we need to recognize what passions God has laid on our hearts. We must determine if what compels us is to please God or to satisfy our own desires.

God has and continues to prepare us for our good works. Remember what Paul told us in Ephesians:

61

> For we are his workmanship, created in Christ Jesus
> for good works, which God prepared beforehand, that
> we should walk in them. (Ephesians 2:10)

Although we know others may have similar skills and gifts, God will give us unique opportunities no one else has to serve others. When we recognize these opportunities with the aid of the Holy Spirit, we will glorify God in all he's prepared us to do.

Every morning, as we begin our walk with God, we have the opportunity to pray for the opportunities he will give us to bless others in his name during the day. If we seek these opportunities, we will find them and achieve God's intended purpose for our lives.

QUESTIONS FOR THOUGHT

Man's chief end is to glorify God and enjoy him forever. How do
we glorify God?_____

_____

_____

_____

What can you do to glorify God you are not doing today?

_____

_____

_____

_____

God has equipped you to perform the good deeds he has assigned
to you.

Describe the personality God has given you. _____

_____

_____

_____

What are your abilities and aptitudes? _____

_____

_____

What are your spiritual gifts? _____

_____

_____

_____

_____

What are your passions? _____

_____

_____

_____

_____

_____

CHAPTER EIGHT

CALL TO ACTION—EVANGELISM

Evangelism is sharing the love of God and the gospel of Jesus Christ with an unsaved person/people to provide the opportunity for them to respond to God's call and to receive God's offer of eternal life with him. Our motivation for evangelism should be our love for our fellow man and concern for their eternal destiny.

THE GOSPEL

The gospel is a message about who God is, and that we are his creation—created to love him, to worship him, and to serve him as an act of love.

The gospel is a message about sin that tells us we have fallen far short of who God wants us to become, and that our sin places us under his condemnation. We are told there is nothing we are capable of doing that will make us right with God and bring us back into God's favor. Of great importance is that unless and until we see our sin as an offense against God, we do not see our actions as sin at all.

The gospel is a message about Jesus that tells us Jesus, God the Son, because of his great love for us ,came to earth to save sinners from God's judgment and punishment. We are told Jesus died on the cross as an atonement for our sins. We are told of Jesus's resurrection, of his ascension back to heaven, and that he now sits at the right hand of the Father.

As we think about and share the gospel, we must be careful to present Jesus and not just his saving work. The object of our faith is Jesus. When we share the gospel with the unsaved world, we should first share who Jesus is, and then what he accomplished on our behalf.

OUR THREEFOLD PREPARATION

PRAYER: First we need to pray about those to whom we are to take the message of the gospel. We must have God's leading and the aid of the Holy Spirit to determine who and why and where we share Jesus's message.

ARMOR OF GOD: When we take the gospel to the world, we need to put on the whole armor of God to be protected in spiritual warfare against the powers of the prince of darkness. Satan does not want us to bring others into the light. But God has given us the capability through the power of the Holy Spirit to persevere.

> Therefore take up the whole armor of God, that you may be able to withstand in the evil day, and having done all, to stand firm. Stand therefore, having fastened on the belt of truth, and having put on the breastplate of righteousness, and, as shoes for your feet, having put on the readiness given by the gospel of peace. In all circumstances take up the shield of faith, with which you can extinguish all the flaming darts of the evil one; and take the helmet of salvation, and the sword of the Spirit, which is the word of God, praying at all times in the Spirit, with all prayer and supplication. (Eph. 6:13-18a)

"In a sense the 'whole armor of God' is a picture of Jesus Christ. Christ is the Truth (John 14:6), and he is our righteousness (2 Corinthians 5:21) and our peace (Ephesians 2:14). His faithfulness makes possible our faith (Galatians 2:20); he is our salvation (Luke 2:30); and he is the Word of God (John 1:1,14). This means that when we trusted Christ, we received the armor … We are never out of reach of Satan's devices, so we must never be without the whole armor of God."[2]

CHRISTLIKE COMPASSION: How would we describe Jesus? Not just what he accomplished during his ministry on earth or the theological significance of what he accomplished, but also who he is. I've discovered there is one descriptive word that tells us something about who he is and what it is about him in his interaction with people that we are to emulate. I believe the word we are looking for is compassion. Compassion is the one personal characteristic almost exclusively used to describe Jesus in the gospels.

> And Jesus went throughout all the cities and villages, teaching in their synagogues and proclaiming the gospel of the kingdom and healing every disease and every affliction. When he saw the crowds, he had **compassion** for them, because they were harassed and helpless, like sheep without a shepherd. (Matt 9:35-36)
>
> When he went ashore he saw a great crowd, and he had **compassion** on them and healed their sick (Matt 14:14)

---

2 Wiersbe, W. W. (1996, c1989). *The Bible Exposition Commentary.* "An exposition of the New Testament comprising the entire 'BE' series"–Jkt. (Eph 6:13). (Victor Books, Wheaton, Ill.:) .

"I have **compassion** on the crowd, because they have been with me now three days and have nothing to eat. And if I send them away hungry to their homes, they will faint on the way." (Matt 15:32)

And Jesus stopped and called to them and said, "What do you want me to do for you?" They said to him, "Lord, we want our eyes to be opened." Moved with **compassion**, Jesus touched their eyes, and immediately they regained their sight and followed him. (Matt 20:32-34)

When he went ashore he saw a great crowd, and he had **compassion** on them, because they were like sheep without a shepherd. And he began to teach them many things. (Mark 6:34)

As he drew near to the gate of the town, behold, a man who had died was being carried out, the only son of his mother, and she was a widow, and a considerable crowd from the town was with her. And when the Lord saw her, he had **compassion** on her and said to her, "Do not weep." Then he came up and touched the bier, and the bearers stood still. And he said, "Young man, I say to you, arise." (Luke 7:12-14)

Compassion is defined in the dictionary as a feeling of deep sympathy and sorrow for another who is stricken by misfortune, accompanied by a strong desire to alleviate the suffering. The Greek word for compassion is *splanchnizomai* and provides us with an even deeper understanding of what the gospel writers were telling us about Jesus. This word describes what happens to a person when their intestines are tied up in emotional knots—a pain that settles deep in the gut. Compassion describes what you feel when you experience something that causes you to say "That tears me apart inside."

Because of Jesus's compassion for us, we have a Savior who was willing to suffer and die on the cross for our sins. A Savior with deep compassion who desires to shower us with his grace and mercy as an act of love.

As Pastor Ike Reighard related, "Jesus-like compassion can be described with the acronym **SALT:** [This describes what we need to do to have Christlike compassion.]

SALT

See people the way Jesus saw them;
Accept people the way Jesus accepted them;
Love people the way Jesus loved them;
Touch people the way Jesus touched them.[3]

Only with Christlike compassion as a Spirit-driven motivation will our evangelistic outreach truly and completely honor God. Let us pray God gives us a full measure of Jesus-like compassion for people who are hurting spiritually, emotionally, and/or physically.

GO MAKE DISCIPLES

Our love affair with God should become the motivation for all our relationships with others—not only with our family and close friends but with everyone we meet.

> Now the eleven disciples went to Galilee, to the mountain to which Jesus had directed them. And when they saw him they worshiped him, but some doubted.

---

3 Ike Reighard in conversation with Chris Rivers on the *Culture Bus*, 3 Nov 2014

> And Jesus came and said to them, "All authority in heaven and on earth has been given to me. Go therefore and make disciples of all nations, baptizing them in the name of the Father and of the Son and of the Holy Spirit, teaching them to observe all that I have commanded you. And behold, I am with you always, to the end of the age." (Matthew 28:16-20)

Jesus told the disciples to "go and make disciples of all nations." The word "go" in the Greek is in the present perfect tense and could be more accurately translated "while going." The disciples would understand Jesus to be telling them to make disciples wherever they went in their daily life—this is what Jesus is telling us as well.

When people observe us and witness our love for God, some of them will want to also experience their own loving relationship with him. Loving God is where our contribution to evangelism should begin, and then we can take advantage of the opportunities God gives us to share the gospel.

> Always be prepared to give an answer to everyone who asks you to give the reason for the hope that you have. But do this with gentleness and respect. (1 Peter 3:15b)

QUESTIONS FOR THOUGHT

Give examples of times you have had Christlike compassion for someone. _____ _____

_____

_____

_____

What did you do as a result of your compassion? _____

_____

_____

_____

What else could you have done? _____

_____

_____

_____

What do you need to do to prepare yourself to share God's love in a fallen world? _____

_____

_____

_____

_____

_____

What is your reason for the hope that you have?_____

_____

_____

_____

_____

_____

_____

_____

EPILOGUE:

OUR LEGACY: WHAT REALLY MATTERS?

An inheritance is what we leave *for* others. A legacy is what we leave *in* them. Our legacy is what lives on through others after we die.

Dr. Johnny Parker in his book *Turn the Page* describes the need to live our lives with an endgame foresight:

> Examining our story (our life) through the lens of death can help shape and define our paths and can help bring to the surface what's stirring in our hearts. In fact, at the risk of sounding morbid, one of the exercises I assign to the CEOs I work with is to write their obituaries.
>
> I first realized the power of this perspective when I was about to turn forty and asked myself a heart-centric question, "If I were on my deathbed this very minute, looking back over the course of my life, how would I know if I'd been successful?" From that vantage point, I realized that I would most certainly measure my success based on the quality of my relationships, starting with my bride, our sons, our family, and close friends. And suddenly everything was clear. If at the end of my story, I am going to measure my success by the quality of my relationships, then this mission, this

question, this "why" needs to define the story I choose
to live today.[4]

What would your and my obituary say if we were to die today?
What would we like it to say? We still have time to have our
obituary describe a life lived sharing our love for our Lord, and
our love and compassion for everyone God puts in our path.

How will you and I finish?

In the genealogy from Adam to Noah that is found in Genesis
5, all the lives listed ended with the phrase "he died" except for
what was written about Enoch:

> When Enoch had lived 65 years, he fathered
> Methuselah. Enoch walked with God after he fathered
> Methuselah 300 years and had other sons and
> daughters. Thus all the days of Enoch were 365 years.
> Enoch walked with God, and he was not, for God
> took him. (Genesis 5:21-24)

> By faith Enoch was taken up so that he should not see
> death, and he was not found, because God had taken
> him. Now before he was taken he was commended as
> having pleased God. And without faith it is impossible
> to please him, for whoever would draw near to God
> must believe that he exists and that he rewards those
> who seek him. (Hebrews 11:5-6)

Using my sanctified imagination, I see Enoch walking with God
experiencing a deep love. They are having a great time talking

---

4 Dr. Johnny Parker, *Turn the Page*, (Elk Lake Publishing, Inc., 2017),
p. 81-82

and laughing as they walk along together. Then God says (in my imagination) to Enoch, "We are having such a good time, let's continue our walk and conversation in heaven." And then Enoch was not (on earth).

If we love God and have faith like Enoch's, our step from earth to heaven will be a small one, because we will already be walking with God.

Questions for Thought

Write the obituary you would want to have written to describe
your life. _____

_____

_____

_____

_____

_____

_____

What do you need to change to make the obituary a reality?

_____

_____

_____

_____

_____

_____

ATTACHMENT 1

GOD IS TRANSCENDENT

ETERNAL

"I am the Alpha and the Omega," says the Lord God, "who is and who was and who is to come, the Almighty. (Revelation 1:8)

INCOMPREHENSIBLE

Oh, the depth of the riches and wisdom and knowledge of God! How unsearchable are his judgments and how unscrutable his ways! (Romans 11:33)

"For my thoughts are not your thoughts, neither are your ways my ways," declares the LORD, "For as the heavens are higher than the earth, so are my ways higher than your ways and my thoughts than your thoughts." (Isaiah 55:8-9)

OMNIPRESENT—ALWAYS PRESENT

"Am I a God at hand," declares the LORD, "and not a God far away? Can a man hide himself in secret places so that I cannot see him?" declares the LORD. Do I not fill heaven and earth?" declares the LORD. (Jeremiah 23:23-24)

And no creature is hidden from his sight, but all are naked and exposed to the eyes of him to whom we must give account. (Hebrews 4:13)

Omnicient—All-Knowing

O LORD, you have searched me and known me! You know when I sit down and when I rise up; you discern my thoughts from afar. You search out my path and my lying down and are acquainted with all my ways. Even before a word is on my tongue, behold, O LORD, you know it altogether. You hem me in behind and before, and lay your hand upon me. Such knowledge is too wonderful for me; it is high; I cannot attain it. (Psalm 139:1-6)

Oh, the depth of the riches and wisdom and knowledge of God! How unsearchable are his judgments and how unscrutable his ways! (Romans 11:33)

Sovereign—All-Powerful

Then Job answered the LORD and said:
"I know that you can do all things, and that no purpose of yours can be thwarted." (Job 42:1-2)

Infinite—God is not confined to the finiteness of space and time

But will God indeed dwell on the earth? Behold, heaven and the highest heaven cannot contain you; how much less this house that I have built! (1 Kings 8:27)

Invisible—God is Spirit

To the King of the ages, immortal, invisible, the only God, be honor and glory forever and ever. Amen. (1 Timothy 1:17)

God is spirit, and those who worship him must worship in spirit and truth. (John 4:24)

Holy, Holy, Holy—The Trisagion, a Hebrew language form of emphasis

> And one called out to another and said:
> "Holy, Holy, Holy is the LORD of hosts;
> the whole earth is full of his glory." (Isaiah 6:3)

> "Holy, holy, holy, is the LORD God Almighty, who was and is and is to come! (Revelation 4:8b)

> But as he who called you is holy, you also be holy in all your conduct, since it is written, "You shall be holy, for I am holy." (1 Peter 1:15)

GOD IS RELATIONAL

LOVING

> "For God so loved the world, that he gave his only Son, that whoever believes in him should not perish but have eternal life." (John 3:16)

> Beloved, let us love one another, for love is from God, and whoever loves has been born of God and knows God. Anyone who does not love does not know God, because God is love. (1 John 4:7-8)

GOOD

> Praise the LORD!
> Oh, give thanks to the LORD, for he is good,
> for his steadfast love endures forever. (Psalm 106:1)

> The LORD is good,
> a stronghold in the day of trouble;
> he knows those who take refuge in him. (Nahum 1:7)

FAITHFUL

> Know therefore that the LORD your God is God, the faithful God who keeps covenant and steadfast love with those who love him and keep his commandments, to a thousand generations. (Deuteronomy 7:9)

GRACIOUS

> And God is able to make all grace abound to you, so that having all sufficiency in all things at all times, you may abound in every good work. (2 Corinthians 9:8)

LONG-SUFFERING

> The LORD passed before him and proclaimed, "The LORD, the LORD, a God merciful and gracious, slow to anger, and abounding in steadfast love and faithfulness, keeping steadfast love for thousands, forgiving iniquity and transgression and sin, but who will by no means clear the guilty, visiting the iniquity of the fathers on the children and the children's children, to the third and the fourth generation." (Exodus 34:6-7)

MERCIFUL

> What shall we say then? Is there injustice on God's part? By no means! For he says to Moses, "I will have mercy on whom I have mercy, and I will have compassion on whom I have compassion." So then it depends not on human will or exertion, but on God, who has mercy. (Romans 9:14-16)

JUST

> Righteousness and justice are the foundation of your throne;
>   steadfast love and faithfulness go before you. (Psalm 89:14)

ATTACHMENT 2

PERSONALITY

As noted on page 51, every person has a unique personality although we may share some characteristics. To determine your personality, we recommend the "Wired That Way Personality Profile," which includes a test, scoring sheet, and explanation of the various personality types. Taking this test will help you figure out who you are from a personality standpoint.

Other personality assessments are the Myers-Briggs Type Indicator (MBTI), the Enneagram, the DISC assessment, and dozens more.

To give you an example of the "Wired That Way Personalities"— the four different personality types are the Popular Sanguine, the Powerful Choleric, the Perfect Melancholy, and the Peaceful Phlegmatic.

POPULAR SANGUINE:

Basic Desire: Have Fun

Emotional Needs:

> Attention
> Affection
> Approval
> Acceptance

Controls By: Charm

Popular Sanguines, like Powerful Cholerics, tend to lead and are extroverted, opportunistic, and outspoken. Like Peaceful

Phlegmatics, they like to play and are witty, easygoing, and not goal oriented.

POWERFUL CHOLERIC

Basic Desire: Have Control

Emotional Needs:

>Loyalty
>Sense of Control
>Appreciation
>Credit for Work

Controls By: Threat of Anger

Besides the characteristics shared with Popular Sanguines, they also share traits with Perfect Melancholies. They are driven by work, are decisive, organized, and goal oriented.

PERFECT MELANCHOLY

Basic Desire: Have Perfection

Emotional Needs:

>Sensitivity
>Support
>Space
>Silence

Controls By: Threat of Moods

Perfect Melancholies share traits with Powerful Cholerics and also Peaceful Phlegmatics. They analyze, are introverted, pessimistic, and soft-spoken.

Peaceful Phlegmatic

Basic Desire: Have Peace

Emotional Needs:

> Peace and Quiet
> Feeling of worth
> Lack of Stress
> Respect

Controls By: Procrastination

Peaceful Phlegmatics are the peacemakers among the personalities as the name would lead you to believe. They make good friends, are good workers, and are good at smoothing over troubled waters.

Most people are a blend of two touching personalities. I (Roy) am a Choleric with just enough Melancholy to drive Deb crazy. Deb is a Choleric-Sanguine with Choleric strengths and sanguine weaknesses.

Learning your personality style and how to recognize others' styles will help you be the loving friend or neighbor the situation calls for. Mirroring their personality needs in your conversation will help communication take place.

While each of us is one type or a blend of two, Jesus was a blend of all four—having all the strengths of each personality and none of the weaknesses.

ATTACHMENT 3

APTITUDE TESTS

As mentioned, there are thousands of different apptitude tests that measure just about everything from verbal skills to math to mechanical to engineering. Several companies which offer such assessments are listed below:

Berke Assessment: https://www.berkeassessment.com

What Career is Right for Me?

https://www.whatcareerisrightforme.com/career-aptitude-test.php

Criteria Testing: https://www.criteriacorp.com/solution/aptitude.php

1-2-3 Test: https://www.123test.com/career-test/

ATTACHMENT 4

SPIRITUAL GIFTS TESTING

There are many spiritual gifts assessments available as well. Here are links to four.

1. https://spiritualgiftstest.com/spiritual-gifts-test-adult-version/

2. Team Ministry: https://gifts.churchgrowth.org/spiritual-gifts-survey/

3. http://giftstest.com/

4. https://mintools.com/spiritual-gifts-test.htm

ABOUT THE AUTHORS

Roy Haggerty is a lover of God, a husband, and a father. He has taught Bible studies for over twenty-five years. Roy retired in his mid-sixties and has spent his time immersed in Bible study and a study of modern politics. He has taken courses towards a masters of theology through Reformed Theological Seminary.

He grew up in Massachusetts and graduated from Thayer Academy. He attended Kemper Military Junior College, Booneville, MO, before transferring to and graduating from the University of Miami, Miami, FL, with a major in history and a minor in economics. During the Vietnam War, Roy volunteered for the US Air Force and spent eighteen months in the Middle East as a staff-sergeant assigned to the AF Security Service.

Roy worked for Southern Bell in Ft. Lauderdale, FL, and had several assignments at AT&T Headquarters in New Jersey. Promoted to Division Manager-IT Operations, Roy managed the rollout of the company's marketing management system.

Roy left AT&T for a position as Senior Vice President & COO for Computer Horizons Corp.

Hired by Adecco to become President and CEO of Ajilon IT Services, Roy, over his seventeen years tenure, grew the organization from a regional company with eight offices and $49M in sales, to an international company with sixty-six offices and over $1B in sales.

Contact Roy at Roy@RoyHaggerty.com, on Facebook as Roy Haggerty, and on LinkedIn at RoyHaggerty.

Deb Haggerty is a lover of God, a wife, and a mother. Born in Benson, Minnesota, she graduated from Macalester College, St. Paul, MN, in 1969 with a BA in English Literature and a minor in music and religion.

Deb worked for Southern Bell and AT&T for thirteen years, holding positions from non-management to district level management. While at Southern Bell, she completed an MBA in Human Resources Management and Organizational Design.

She left AT&T in 1985 to found Positive Connections®, a management consulting and training firm. After successfully battling breast cancer in 2000, she started a website to encourage others on that path, PositiveHope.com. 2010 saw the start of her Christian book review site, PositiveGrace.com. In 2016, she purchased Elk Lake Publishing, Inc. (https://elklakepublishinginc.com), a Christian publishing company.

Deb teaches at many Christian writers' conferences, has been published in over twenty books, and has over fifty articles to her credit. She loves talking with groups about her relationship with Jesus Christ.

She can be found on Facebook as Deb Ogle Haggerty, @DebHaggerty on Twitter, and DebHaggerty on LinkedIn.

Roy and Deb live on beautiful Boot Pond just outside Plymouth, Massachusetts, with Coki the Dog, their adorable miniature dachshund.

BIBLIOGRAPHY

Anderson, Neil. Adapted from *Living Free in Christ*. Bethany Books. Bloomington, MN 2001.

Batterson, Mark. *Soulprint*. Multinomah Books. Colorado Springs, CO. 2015. p. 3.

Brown, Steve. "Steve's Letter—Perverting God," *Key Life Newsletter*. June 6, 2018.

Haggerty, Roy. "Edwards on Free Will" 1990. p. 11

Littauer, Florence and Marita. "Wired That Way Personality Plan." © 2006. Revell version 2015. Revell, a Division of Baker Books. Ada, MI.

Myers, Bill. *The Jesus Experience*. Shiloh Run Press. Ulrichsville, OH. 2015. pp. 49-57.

New Bible Dictionary. Second Edition. Tyndale House Publishers, Inc. Carol, IL. 1962. p. 711.

Packer, J. I. *Keep in Step with the Spirit*. Revell. Revell, a Division of Baker Books. Ada, MI. 1984. p. 49, 110.

Parker, Dr. Johnny. *Turn the Page*. Elk Lake Publishing, Inc. 2017. p. 81-82

Reighard, Ike. In conversation with Chris Rivers on the *Culture Bus*. 3 Nov 2014.

Tozer, A.W. *The Knowledge of the Holy.* New York: HarperCollins. New York, NY. 1961. p. 1.

Westminster Shorter Catechism, Free Presbyterian Publications. Lawrenceville, GA. 1985. p. 287.

Wiersbe, W. W. (1996, c1989). *The Bible Exposition Commentary.* "An exposition of the New Testament comprising the entire 'BE' series"–Jkt. (Eph 6:13). Victor Books. Wheaton, IL.

Zondervan NASB Study Bible. "Major Covenants of the Old Testament." Zondervan. Nashville, TN. 1999. p. 16.

RESOURCES FOR ADDITIONAL STUDY

Be the Miracle, Delores Liesner

Evangelism & the Sovereignty of God, J. I. Packer

Keep in Step with the Spirit, J. I. Packer

Living Free in Christ, Neil Anderson

Personality Plus, Florence and Marita Littauer

Pure-Hearted, Kathy Collard Miller

Soulprint, Mark Batterson

The Deeper Life, Daniel Henderson

The Jesus Experience, Bill Myers

The Knowledge of the Holy, A. W. Tozer

The Sailboat and the Sea and Study Guide, Peter Lundell

Turn the Page: Unlocking the Story within You, Dr. Johnny Parker

NOTES

NOTES

NOTES

NOTES

NOTES

NOTES

NOTES

NOTES

50489646R00066

Made in the USA
Middletown, DE
25 June 2019